Physiotherapist, Physical Therapist

A Career Guide

Job Description, Qualifications, Salary, Training, Education Requirements, Positions, Disciplines, Resume, Career Outlook, and Much More!!

By: Christopher Wright

Copyrights and Trademarks

This publication is Copyright © 2013. All products, graphics, publications, software and services mentioned and recommended in this publication are protected by trademarks. In such instance, all trademarks & copyright belong to the respective owners.

Disclaimer and Legal Notice

This product is not legal, medical, or accounting advice and should not be interpreted in that manner. You need to do your own due-diligence to determine if the content of this product is right for you. While every attempt has been made to verify the information shared in this publication, neither the author, neither publisher, nor the affiliates assume any responsibility for errors, omissions or contrary interpretation of the subject matter herein. Any perceived slights to any specific person(s) or organization(s) are purely unintentional.

We have no control over the nature, content and availability of the web sites listed in this book. The inclusion of any web site links does not necessarily imply a recommendation or endorse the views expressed within them. We take no responsibility for, and will not be liable for, the websites being temporarily unavailable or being removed from the internet.

The accuracy and completeness of information provided herein and opinions stated herein are not guaranteed or warranted to produce any particular results, and the advice and strategies, contained herein may not be suitable for every individual. Neither the author nor the publisher shall be liable for any loss incurred as a consequence of the use and application, directly or indirectly, of any information presented in this work. This publication is designed to provide information in regard to the subject matter covered.

Neither the author nor the publisher assume any responsibility for any errors or omissions, nor do they represent or warrant that the ideas, information, actions, plans, suggestions contained in this book is in all cases accurate. It is the reader's responsibility to find advice before putting anything written in this book into practice. The information in this book is not intended to serve as legal, medical, or accounting advice.

Foreword

The fact that you have landed on this page is proof enough of your interest in the field of physiotherapy. Well, we agree with your choice considering the growth opportunities that this field has to offer amidst of uncertain economy and joblessness.

According to the Bureau of Labor statistics US department of labor, the physiotherapy sector is expected to experience and employment growth of 39%. This is even higher than the average employment growth of 14%.

If you are still perplexed and unsure as to what career you should opt for, keep on reading this book and you will surely find your answer.

From the basics of physiotherapy to the educational requirements, standard pay structure, career progression and fields of specialization; this book tells you all you need to know to become a physiotherapist. It even elaborates the examples, statistics and information pertaining to different states and nations.

From the time you start considering the possibility of becoming a physical therapist up till you take retirement, this book will serve as your expert guide throughout your journey of physical therapy. Keep on reading and find a way to reach the top ladder in physiotherapy.

Best of Luck!!

Acknowledgements

I would like to express my gratitude towards my family, friends, and colleagues for their kind co-operation and encouragement which helped me in completion of this book.

My thanks and appreciations go to my colleagues and people who have willingly helped me out with their abilities.

Table of Contents

Chapter 1: Physiotherapy – An Overview

According to the definition by the Australian Physiotherapy Association,

"Physiotherapy is a healthcare profession that assesses, diagnoses, treats, and works to prevent disease and disability through physical means. Physiotherapists are experts in movement and function who work in partnership with their patients, assisting them to overcome movement disorders, which may have been present from birth, acquired through accident or injury, or are the result of ageing or life-changing events"

Physiotherapy is a British term for physical therapy, abbreviated as PT. Both of these terms will be used interchangeably in this book. The meaning and all other basic aspects remains the same.

Elaborating the above definition, Physiotherapy, or physical therapy is a branch of clinical health science that deals with bodily pain and movement disorders. It does so by employing several physical and natural procedures such as massage, exercise and stretching etcetera.

But this is just a basic definition. Physical therapy is much more vast and extensive than this. It contains several branches and specializations.

It requires lots of determination, hard work and patience to become a physical therapist. However, the rewards are also fabulous and worth all the efforts.

Physiotherapy is a highly paid and respected profession. Moreover, the fact that physical therapists help other people in improving their lifestyle and get rid of bodily pains makes it a service to humanity. The inner satisfaction that you get after being a physiotherapist complements the high salary and respect that one gets in this profession.

The study of physiotherapy includes study of subjects that will help the person develop skills and patience required to diagnose, treat, prevent, rehabilitate and educate the patients with physical disabilities. It primarily includes study of anatomy, physiology and neuroscience.

Moreover, it is a compulsory requirement for physical therapists to get registered by law. The licensure and registration requirements vary across different states and nations and are explained in detail later on in this book.

This field of medicine requires you to work in both, hospitals and community healthcare systems.

Well, this was just a brief summary of the underlying profession. Let's move forward and explore as to what actually is the role and job description of a physiotherapist.

What Physiotherapists Do?

Before we move on to how you can become a physical therapist, let's see what actually will you be required to do once you become a physiotherapist. Like every other profession, this one has certain demands that you need to fulfill.

Physical therapist, also known as 'movement specialists' analyze and treat a number of bodily ailments that affects the normal movements of the body. For example, orthopedists mostly suggest regular physical therapy to patients having osteoarthritis, back pain, rheumatoid arthritis, spinal pain, spinal stenosis, Parkinson's disease and several other long term health problems.

The role of physical therapists differs according to their experience, position, specialization and most importantly the individual needs of the patients. However there are common functions that fall under the job description of every physiotherapist.

PTs all over the world are expected to know and perform the following tasks apart from their specialized job description.

- Assess the condition of the patient, diagnose and recommend appropriate treatment.

- Treat the patient using a range of techniques according to his/her condition. Some of the common physiotherapy techniques include joint manipulation, soft tissue mobilization, acupuncture, hydrotherapy and several other exercise programs

- PTs are required to know the appropriate and safe usage of treatment devices like ultrasound, electrotherapy, ice and heat packs.

- Train the patients on how to use movement aid devices such as walking frames, calipers, splints, crutches and wheelchairs.

- Teach patients exercises that they can perform on their own.

- Educate them on the prevention of bodily ailments and injuries.

- Develop an appropriate fitness program with the patient to prevent the loss of mobility

- Develop, implement and promote fitness and wellness programs for the community

And most importantly, keep the patient motivated and optimistic toward life.

Scope of Work

As already said, the scope of physiotherapy is not limited to the above mentioned tasks. Physical therapists are experts in the assessment and treatment of neuromuscular, cardiothoracic and musculoskeletal problems. These are ailments that affect the physical functionality and ability of individuals to move the way they want.

These problems can occur at any stage of life. This implies that physical therapy is not just for one gender or age group. From infants to old age retired people, physiotherapy has scope and importance in every stage of life.

Here are some of the health issues pertaining to different age groups that require physiotherapy treatment.

Infancy: Baby Torticollis

Torticollis refers to the retraction of the sternocleidomastoid muscle which is a very common issue in new born babies. It makes it difficult for them to move their head from one side to other. Since a newly born baby's skull is very soft, flexible and susceptible to alterations, sleeping on one side leads to a flattened head, called positional plagiocephaly in medical terms.

Torticollis normally happens because of the position taken by the infants in their last few weeks in uterus. Not every time, but Torticollis often leads to permanent deformity of the skull. This is where physiotherapy comes in the scene.

Physical therapists use soft tissue message and several other exercises to loosen the muscles in the baby's neck. They teach the baby to turn their head to put equal pressure on both sides of the skull.

Childhood: Neuromotor Delay

A child taking too long to sit, crawl or walk is an example of neuromotor delay. Though there is not any specific time as to when the child should start performing these activities. However, there is a standard range of weeks for these functions. For example, a 2 year old child unable to walk unaided is not normal. Pediatric therapists are experts in assessing and treating such issues.

Teenage: Bone Fracture in Arms or Legs

Now this is something very common among teenagers. They are very susceptible to bone fractures. While the fractures are treated by orthopedists, physical therapists ensure that the affected bone is healed and strengthened. They make the kids do exercises that will bring back the mobility, flexibility and strength in the fractured part.

Youngsters: Sprains and Sports Injuries

Sprain in the ankle during the dance class, while playing football or running across the stairs to catch the train are some of the common happenings in a youngster's life which make them pay frequent visits to the physical therapists.

Physiotherapists play a very important role in the life of youngsters. This age group is very active and unwilling to sit at home. Moreover, they can't afford to miss their school and other important activities.

It puts on extra effort on the physical therapists to make sure that they return to their normal routine in the shortest possible time. This also implies that physical therapists develop a short fitness program that they can follow regularly in their busy life to minimize the reoccurrence of the injury.

Pregnant Women: Back Pain

Back pain is a common characteristic of pregnancy. This is due to the fact that the growing weight of the baby induces change in the bodily posture. The pregnancy hormones loosen the ligaments causing the joints in the back to move more than usual. This in turn weakens the joint support and causes low back pain.

Physical therapists are experts in dealing with pregnancy back pains. They train the pregnant women several exercises that strengthen their joints and reduce the back pain.

Mid life: Heart Diseases

Heart diseases can be caused by a large number of factors, some of which can be addressed by physiotherapy. It is part of a physiotherapist's job to develop exercise programs for managing weight, cholesterol and blood pressure levels. Cardiac rehabilitation program and counseling on smoking cessation also falls under the head of physiotherapy.

Old Age: Osteoporosis

Old age brings with it quite a number of ailments, osteoporosis being one of them. It is very common among the elderly. It is a condition where the bones get brittle and weak, which in turn affects the structure of bones and bodily posture. Stooped back is a sign of osteoporosis.

Physiotherapy is the best way to reduce the pain associated with osteoporosis. In such cases, a physical therapist develops a comprehensive treatment program including bone strengthening exercises, diet plan, aerobics and massages.

Summing up this section, physiotherapy is not a monotonous, age specific or gender specific job, neither is it limited to a few diseases. It has scope in all age groups, professions, genders and aspects of life.

Work Environment

Now that you know the variety of work that you will be doing after becoming a physical therapist, here is the next surprise for you. The working conditions will also be equally diverse.

As indicated in the previous section, physiotherapy has a vast range of applications. This field of medical science extends from acute care to prevention of immobility, health care, training and awareness, fitness programs, chronic disease management and occupational health.

The vast scope of physiotherapy implies a diverse variety of working conditions for the physiotherapists that depends upon the facilities of the health care and needs of the individual patients.

For example, children especially those with learning difficulties require a different approach and treatment. Rehabilitation cannot always be done in a hospital.

Being a physical therapist, you might have your own office or working desk, but your clinic or hospital is not the only place where you are going to perform treatments. Some treatments would require you to visit the patient's place or fitness center, sports club or any other communal rehabilitation center.

The varying working conditions coupled with the diverse set of responsibilities keep this job interesting.

How Much Do Physiotherapists Earn?

Every state and healthcare facility has a different pay package for physiotherapists. The salary depends upon several factors such as qualifications, experience, successful cases etcetera. However, the average salary of physical therapists is higher than the average income of an individual.

According to the U.S. Bureau of Labor Statistics,

- On average a physical therapist earn $72,790 per year

- Majority of the PTs earn between $60,300 and $85,540 annually

- Only 10 percent of Physical Therapists earn less than $50,350 per year.

- Approximately 10% of PTs earn more than $104,350 per year.

PTs that are employed in nursing care units, home health care facilities and private clinics earn more than the average salary of a physical therapist.

According to the American Physical Therapy Association (APTA), at the moment there are more the 184,000 physical therapists licensed under the US law. The median salary quoted by APTA is $80,000 per year which is slightly higher than the one quoted by the U.S. Bureau of Labor Statistics.

Besides the US, physiotherapists are highly paid in the UK as well.

- A recently qualified physiotherapist can expect to earn £21,176 - £27,625 per year in the National Health Service (NHS).

- Specialist physiotherapists earn between £25,528 - £34,189.

- Advanced physiotherapists earn between £30,460 - £40,157

Australia is very generous when it comes to the salary of physiotherapists.

- The average starting salary of a physiotherapist in Australia is AU$ 50,500 on an annual basis.

- The average salary of physiotherapists in Australia is AU$ 77,002 per year.

- Majority of the physiotherapists in Australia earn between AU$ 47,949 - AU$ 88,111.

- The hourly pay of physiotherapists starts from AU$ 21.58 and can go as high as AU$ 51, depending upon the years of experience.

Job Outlook

While salary is definitely an important factor to consider when thinking over the possible career choices, even more important is the job outlook.

We live in an uncertain economy. You never know what will be the price of chicken and bread after 10 years, and will your current salary be enough to support that. Salary is important for your present and job outlook is essential for your future.

Exploring an occupation according to its job outlook is indeed a feasible and safe option. It is a forecast of what an employment will be like in future. Taking a note of job outlook is helpful as it will help you predict your chances of getting a good, lucrative job in the future.

Physiotherapy has a pretty bright future and a strong job outlook. According to the U.S. Bureau of Labor Statistics, the field of physical therapy is growing at an exceptionally high rate. It is estimated that by 2018, the field would have grown by 30%. This is even indicated by the fact that many insurance companies these days are covering physical therapy in the medical insurance.

And same is the story of other nations. The physiotherapy job industry in Australia has grown at an average rate of 20.2% over the past five years and is expected to grow even more in the next 5 years.

It is vital to keep up with the job outlook forecasts, especially if you are looking forward to a lucrative career as a physiotherapist. In order to estimate job outlook, look up to the economists of the US Bureau of Labor Statistics Office of Occupational Statistics and Employment Projections. They compare and project the change in employment settings usually over a period of ten years. The projection of change in an occupation is described by saying it will:

- Grow faster than the average occupations

- Grow at a similar pace as average occupations

- Grow at a much faster pace than average occupations

- Have very insignificant change

- Have no change at all

- Is moderately or slowly declining

- Declining rapidly

You may rely on the economists with their forecasted change in an occupation's change because in addition to other important factors, they also compare the number of job openings with the number of job seekers to estimate the prospects of a particular occupation.

Fortunately, the physiotherapist career you are choosing for yourself has a very good job outlook with reference to the US Bureau of Labor Statistics. According to them, the employment in this field will grow faster than the average occupation over the period of ten years.

The decision has been taken considering several impactful factors together with the statistics and growth rate of this particular field, showing prospects the green signal to take up this lucrative career opportunity.

Chapter 2: How to Become a Physiotherapist?

Now that you have already made your mind to become a physiotherapist, know what it takes to become one.

What are the academic requirements necessary for practice?

Well before we jump to the answer, it is important that you learn about the typical work environment and work load for a physical therapist.

Work Environment and Work Load

Physical therapists may practice in a medical office or a hospital setting. They may see patients in any medical setup such as an orthopedic surgery. Typically, the procedure involves a physician too. A physician recommends a physical therapy treatment and physical therapist to a patient and then follows up to assess the progress of the patient on a regular basis after every few courses of the therapy.

A physical therapy setup must have various different types of apparatuses for the rehabilitation of patients. This may include treadmills, mats and weights where physical therapists can perform various recommended exercises with the patients to boost muscle strength, sensory perception and motor skills.

Entry Level Physical Therapy Careers and Required Physical Therapists Skills

With reference to the American Physical Therapy Association, the following are highlighted as the minimum, basic skills required from an entry level physiotherapist:

- Evaluate and review all physical systems as required to determine the need for physiotherapist services.

- Assess the scope of physical therapy keeping the limitations of the patient in mind.

- Perform various tests to quantify and characterize sensor integrity (vibration, pressure, cold/hot, dull/sharp, etc) range of motion, reflexes and neuromotor skills.

- Decision making and clinical reasoning to determine a particular diagnosis (the patient's problem) as well as prognosis (expecting improvement in patient in terms of how much and when).

- Using the skills of goal-setting to prepare a plan of care in action.

- Use of wheelchairs, walkers, prosthetics, orthotics and other supportive devices.

- Safety, CPR, first-aid, in case of emergency.

- Tissue massage, manual therapy, manipulation and traction.

- Communication skills to deal with family/patient education, and other professionals for consultations.

- Professional values and skills such as responsibility, compassion, integrity and accountability.

- Practice management skills including coding and billing for appropriate reimbursement, medical records documentation, staff supervision for instance, physical therapy assistance for quality improvement.

It is time to reveal the academic requirements you need to ponder over to take up physiotherapy as a career.

Academic Requirements

A career as a physiotherapist requires at least a bachelor's degree in related field together with clearing the physiotherapist certification exam.

Just like other health careers, the coursework for a career as a physiotherapist mainly emphasizes on the sciences including anatomy, chemistry and biology.

As far as the degree is concerned, you are offered master's level degrees as well as doctorate level degrees. In the United States, it is a must that the school you are getting the certification or degree is accredited by the Commission on Accreditation in Physical Therapy Education (CAPTE).

In the UK, to join a full-time undergraduate program, you must qualify the minimum entry requirements set for all other degree courses. However, since there is a lot of competition, sometimes the minimum requirements are set higher than the standard.

To qualify entry requirements and training for physical therapist, a variety of qualifications are accepted:

In Wales and England, entry level candidates must have three A – C grades in A levels, including biological sciences, and at least five A – C grades at GCSEs. The compulsory subjects for GCSEs include English language, math and a combination of science subjects.

Graduates with bachelor's degree in related discipline are considered eligible for entering in a 2-year masters program for physiotherapy.

The twist is that each course outlines its own set of entry requirements. Applicants should list down their preferable courses and check in detail for the specific details of entry requirements for each course on their list.

Alternative Qualifications

There are various other alternative options available to you in addition to the above mentioned qualification. However, it is always preferred that applicants visit the institution to learn about entry requirements.

The list of alternative qualifications is listed below:

- BTEC National Diploma in Health Studies, Science, with merits/distinction in all specified units.

- HND International Baccalaureate

- Advanced GSVQ/GNVQ in Health and Social Science or Care (In addition, a number of institutions require a biological science subject in A level)

- Appropriate course of Foundation

- Certain Access Courses (learn about the access courses recognized by the individual institution you prefer)

In addition to the academic qualification, the following qualities and skills are required by the admission tutors to qualify potential students:

- Enthusiasm, determination and dedication

- Trustworthiness, honesty and reliability

- Ability and flexibility to work in a team

- Ability to take the initiative

- Tolerance and sensitivity

- Helping and caring

- Good communication skills

In some institutions, they accept applications from applicants who discontinued their full time study lately for any valid reason. However, it is essential that applicants provide evidence of their previous academic study to an appropriate level.

Interview Advice

It is important for the applicants to research carefully on the training course, the futuristic scope of physical therapy practice, long term career opportunities and the significance of the role of healthcare experts and professionals.

In ideal situations, applicants will probably observe the work of a physiotherapist by attending open days that are arranged by the physiotherapy departments in hospitals.

Criminal Records

Criminal records can affect your academic career and application. Applicants with such records are suggested to discuss this matter with the institution's management and admission tutors before applying.

Since physiotherapists' job is to deal with patients of different ages and vulnerabilities, any criminal record should be discussed and disclosed to the authorities.

There is a possibility that due to certain criminal convictions, even successful students may fail to get registration for physiotherapist practice.

Visual Impairments and Disabilities

Applicants with any physical disability are suggested to contact the admission authorities and tutors at the university or institution they are applying. In majority cases, sympathetic considerations will be provided to the applicant, with appropriate and careful assessment of the physical disability to make sure the applicant is in the position to meet the demands of the course.

In the UK, applicants with a visual impairment are eligible to pursue career as a physiotherapist thanks to the support of the Royal National Institute for the Blind.

As far as the training career is concerned, to practice as a professional physiotherapist, it is essential that you register yourself in the state's health and care council. This will vary from country to country.

Generally, to register with the state's health and care council to practice physiotherapy professionally, the applicant is required to complete an approved program in physiotherapy. Such programs are offered by a number of universities in different states.

Typically, the programs are offered on a three and four-year undergraduate degree level. Postgraduate level degrees of 2 years are also available at some universities. Applicants can also look out for part-time courses for physiotherapy in different universities.

The training for physiotherapy involves both theory and clinical experience periods, which involves meeting and working with real patients.

Such training sessions also give chances to students to work with students belonging to other disciplines and departments. This establishes a beneficial foundation for building an effective team, which will play an important role in your practical life.

A typical theory course for physiotherapist will cover pathology, physics, physiology and anatomy.

As an applicant, taking a proper academic course for practicing physiotherapy will help you learn more about psychology, develop good communication skills and gain experience from practical treatment.

Full-Time Degree Programs

Students on full-time degree programs for physiotherapy often share courses and part of their studies with other students enrolled for different clinical courses.

Full-Time (Two Year) Accelerated Courses

Many universities and institutes offer accelerated courses for two years full-time to students to quality as professional physiotherapists. However, this is only available to students who have already graduated in other relevant disciplines. Ideally, students search for such programs because these directly lead to a master's degree.

Part Time Courses

Part-time courses are also offered by a number of reputed universities, primarily to students who are already working as physiotherapist assistants and are employed in a healthcare staff or setting sponsored by professional physiotherapists.

However, there are exceptions to practical experience and one can get admission in part time courses even without practical experience based on current educational status.

Career Progression

Physiotherapy is an allied health care profession and its application can be dated back to ancient times. The Chinese used physiotherapy or massages as a treatment, so did Hippocrates. The profession developed with time and today, physiotherapists help people prevent and treat disabilities and other medical conditions. Some people also use physiotherapy to gain strength and mobility more often after a hospital stay.

Your career in physiotherapy starts with a professional physiotherapy course. A number of universities and recognized educational institutions now offer basic physiotherapy courses after which you can specialize in any one particular area.

To start practicing as a physiotherapist in the UK, you must complete a course approved by the Health and Care Professions Council, (HCPC) and then register with the council. You can choose from 3 and 4 year undergraduate degree programs and continue your study with 2 year post graduate programs. Part-time courses are also available.

Once you register yourself with the HCPC, your training would involve theory as well as clinical experience gained by working with patients. You might get a chance to meet students from other medical disciplines during the course of your training. This brief meeting period could later become a strong foundation for team building.

We have discussed the entry level requirements for undergraduate physiotherapy courses in the UK in the last section and here's a brief recall. In England and Wales, students need to have 3 A level subjects (including biological science) and at least five GCSE subjects with grades A – C. once you complete an undergraduate program, you can go for a 2 year master degree in the subject. A number of alternative qualifications are also available.

Physiotherapy degree programs include a combination of classroom study and a clinical internship. You'll be studying courses related to patient care, physiology, anatomy, exercise physiology, motor control, musculoskeletal system, pharmacology, kinesiology and geriatrics.

Clinical training during the degree program gives students an opportunity to practice physical therapy in a number of locations such as rehabilitation centers, hospitals and orthopedic centers. You will be required to work under the supervision of an experienced physical therapist.

Residency

Some physiotherapists decide to continue their studies after the degree program and enroll in physical therapy residency. A residency program may take up to 12 months to complete.

Residency program allows you to focus on a specific area in the field of physiotherapy. Most common areas of focus include geriatric physiotherapy, sports physiotherapy, neurology and orthopedic physiotherapy. For example, you can go for a residency program in sports physiotherapy or join a residency program related to orthopedic therapy. Residency programs may require you to obtain a license to practice and qualify for specialty training.

Fellowship

Fellowship is also a post professional study program that helps physiotherapist become familiar with a defined area of physiotherapy practice. This learning experience includes focused clinical practice, education and research. Generally, physiotherapist fellowship programs are offered in sports, manual orthopedics and hand movement science.

Specialization

Patients and physicians appreciate the talents of a specialized physical therapist for management of different medical conditions. Many patients are advised to go for physical therapy instead of surgery these days and they prefer to work with a specialized physiotherapist.

A specialized physiotherapist is in a better position to examine the patient and develop a more effective plan of action depending on the particular needs of a patient. Statistics show that specialized physiotherapists get paid well and most patients are "very satisfied" with their work.

You have the opportunity to become certified as clinical specialist in one particular area of physiotherapy practice. Read on to find out more about specialization areas.

Although majority of physiotherapists work in hospitals, a large number of physical therapists are also employed in other settings.

Acute care

Physical therapists are required to work with individuals who are admitted to hospitals for reasons such as illness, accident, surgery or recovery from trauma. Your goal will be to help the patients get medically stable as soon as possible and go home.

Rehabilitation Centers or Hospitals

Rehab centers provide physical therapy to patients to improve their ability to care for themselves. Physical therapy provided to the patient can be intense or moderate depending on the patient's condition.

Nursing home or facility

You are most likely to work with elderly patients looking for long-term nursing care and rehab.

Private or outpatient clinic

This is another common setting you'd come across. Patients visit a physical therapist's clinic or office to address their common orthopedic and neuromuscular complaints.

Sports/ fitness centers

Athletes and other people focused on "staying fit" need physical therapists to prevent injury and promote good health. Here, physical therapists emphasize more on preventing injuries and medical conditions, instead of treating them. Settings include fitness centers, sports training facilities, but aren't limited.

Home Care

You would find physiotherapists who provide care at the patient's home. Majority of the patients are seniors who need help with joint problems and other conditions. Home care is also applicable to young kids with developmental disabilities and other medical conditions that can benefit from physical therapy.

Physiotherapists can work in hospice settings and provide care to patients in the last phase of incurable diseases. Your main goal will be to improve patient's condition and maintain functional abilities for as long as possible. Physical therapists working in hospice settings are also responsible to manage pain.

Workplace and other occupational settings

You'll be surprised to know that large corporations and businesses employ physical therapists to enhance employee health, improve safety and boost productivity in the workplace.

Government agencies

You will be required to provide physical therapy to government employees and this might also include military personnel.

Research Center

Last, physical therapists can work in research centers. In these settings, you will conduct research to improve patient care and come up with ideas to increase the limit and scope of physical therapy.

Fields of Specialization

There are a number of specialty areas in the field of physiotherapy and the upcoming pages present a brief description of some of the most common areas. You can read this section to know more about areas that are most appropriate for you.

Orthopedic Physical Therapy

Orthopedic physical therapists help people recover from orthopedic surgeries. Plus, they also help diagnose, treat and manage injuries and other complaints related to the musculoskeletal system.

You would normally find orthopedic physical therapists actively involved with patients receiving treatment for arthritis, sports injuries, joint conditions and other musculoskeletal injuries. Orthopedic physical therapists normally use joint mobilization techniques, cold packs, hot packs and electrical stimulation to speed up recovery in patients.

As mentioned earlier, orthopedic physical therapy is of great help to people having problems with bones, ligaments, tendons or muscles, i.e. the musculoskeletal system. You should be familiar with the basic anatomy and physiology of the muscle, bones, cartilages, tendons, ligaments, joints and other connective tissue to become a good orthopedic physical therapist.

Muscles are important to keep your bones in place and they also play an important part in movement of your body. Different bones are connected by joints and your body movements are also dependent on the health of your joints and connective tissue.

There are a number of medical conditions that adversely affect the function and effectiveness of your musculoskeletal system. Complex medical issues and injuries related to bones, joints and muscles are handled by orthopedic surgeons and specialist orthopedic physical therapists.

What Orthopedic Physical Therapists Do

As you can guess, orthopedic physical therapists assess, plan and organize programs that help patients overcome joint mobility issues and experience significant improvement in pain and other symptoms.

Here is a brief job description of an orthopedic physical therapist.

- Administer and supervise exercises, massages and other techniques to help manage pain and improve patient's strength.

- Work in collaboration with medical practitioners and design an appropriate exercise program.

- Help a patient stabilize after muscle, joint or bone injury. Orthopedic therapists review patient records to identify problems and evaluate treatment effectiveness.

-Educate the patient about proposed exercise/treatment, its expected benefits and how the therapy will help maintain and restore the physical functioning of the patient.

- Record prognosis and response to the application of physical agents such as cold packs, hot pack, ultraviolet lamps, infrared lamps and ultrasound machines. Orthopedic physical therapists can help patients find best community resources and services related to therapy.

- Educate patients about physical therapy, injury prevention and ways people can improve their health.

- Orthopedic physiotherapists can also be part of research groups and findings to improve physical therapy.

- You will also be required to choose the best treatment plan, solve problems and provide support when it comes to clients and patients.

Specialist orthopedic physiotherapists are very effective at managing and treating patients with musculoskeletal disorders or conditions. In fact patients affected by musculoskeletal disorder represent the largest group treated by orthopedic physiotherapists.

Studies reveal that physiotherapy outpatient services treated and managed 1.9 million adults for the same condition in 2010 – 11. Almost 4.8 million patients had follow up appointments to get their condition cured. It is also seen that acute complaints when managed by orthopedic physiotherapists at early stages are less likely to become chronic and long-lasting.

There are more than 200 different types of musculoskeletal complaints which can be effectively managed by orthopedic physiotherapists. Stats also reveal that lower back pain is one of the most commonly reported problem and 80% of people experience back pain at some time in their life. Most people consult their family physicians or GP's for musculoskeletal disorders and 60% of people absent from work blame musculoskeletal disorders for problems.

Orthopedic physiotherapists manage problems at the earliest stages and this does avoid the need for referral to more expensive secondary care. Some physiotherapists also provide patient information booklets and other useful education resources to help patients improve their health and wellbeing.

Clinical Electrophysiology

Clinical electrophysiology uses electrotherapy and other therapeutic technologies such as electrophysiology and physical agents for physical therapy or patient management. This specialty also involves the use of electromyography (EMG) for evaluation and treatment of common complaints. Some physiotherapists use clinical electrophysiology for wound management and speedy tissue healing.

Basically electromyography or EMG detects the electrical potential generated by the muscle cells when they are activated. The result of electrical or neurological activation is then analyzed by a specialist clinical electrophysiology physical therapist to confirm muscle weakness.

Results of EMG investigation also help differentiate between muscle weakness that occurs due to a neurological disorder and that result of a weak nerve attached to a muscle.

If you specialize in clinical electrophysiology, you'll be involved with:

- Electrophysiology, the study of biological properties of muscles, cells and tissues

- Electrotherapy, the use of electrical energy to speed up recovery or wound healing. You would also study physical agents, i.e. sources of energy that may cause injury or damage to muscles. The list may include temperature extremes, exercise, violent vibration and noise.

- Wound management, how you can manage and treat wounds effectively.

Electrotherapy is one of the most widely researched concepts. Some of the most common applications include:

- Tissue repair

- Enhancement of blood circulation

- Pain management

- Improving joint mobility

- Relaxation of muscle spasms

Before you start your career as a clinical electrophysiology physical therapist, you'll have to complete a postgraduate degree, i.e. Doctor of Physical Therapy. This specialty is a lot more complicated than other physical therapy areas and is not something you could easily dive into.

You can apply for a postgraduate degree once you complete your undergraduate degree. The admission process can vary depending on the university or school you choose for your postgraduate degree.

Your postgraduate degree in clinical electrophysiology is most likely to contain the following courses.

- Physiology

- Electrophysiology

- Musculoskeletal anatomy

- Clinical imaging

- Patient management

- Clinical biomechanics

- Exercise physiology

- Pharmacology

- Neuropathology and neuro-anatomy

- Cardio-pulmonary pathology and management

- Physical therapy based practice

- Gait analysis – measurement of body movement, body mechanics and the activity of muscles

Geriatric Physiotherapy

Geriatric physical therapy or physiotherapy as the name suggests, involves patients who are going through the normal aging process. Your body undergoes a number of physical and physiological changes as you become older.

Seniors often encounter medical complaints such as arthritis, balance disorders, incontinence, osteoporosis and joint mobility issues. Geriatric physical therapists on the other hand specialize in treating and managing these problems to help restore joint mobility, reduce pain and increase fitness in patients.

Geriatric physical therapy over the years has become one of the most widely used strategies for improving balance and strength in older adults.

Most seniors are familiar with geriatric physical therapy as an effective recovery treatment that follows an accident or painful condition such as a stroke. In addition to these reasons, geriatric physical therapy is useful for a number of other reasons such as increasing overall fitness, muscle strength, joint mobility and overall balance.

Yes, physical therapy is quite useful to improve balance and avoid falls, something that is very important to prevent injuries and fractures in older adults.

Unfortunately, large number of physiological changes in bones and muscles lead to loss of bone mineral density in seniors. Older adults are also more prone to problems in maintaining coordination and balance which results in fragility fractures.

Hip, arm, wrist and back fractures are the most common conditions in people over 60 and frequently, injuries and fractures are caused by underlying osteoporosis. Almost 35% of people over 65 years of age experience one or more falls in the UK and the number increases to an alarming 45% in people over 80.

Recurrent fractures and injuries due to falls have become one of the leading causes for increased hospitalization in people aged over 75 years. It is also seen that 50% of seniors who have had a recent fall are more likely to fall again and get injured in the next 12 months.

Fractures have also become a particular concern for older women. Statistics reveal that post menopausal women are more prone to fragility fractures, with hip fractures being the most common.

What Geriatric Physical Therapists Do

- A geriatric PT works with older adults to help them understand the physiological changes that occur with the normal ageing process.

- Specialist geriatric PT develops and evaluates specifically designed exercise program that can prevent further joint injury, life-long disability and restore the patient's functional ability.

- Geriatric physical therapists use exercises and other supportive measures to reduce/manage pain and increase overall fitness of patients.

- Often physical therapists use assistive devices to accomplish things such as improved sensation, joint mobility and greater movement freedom. They also need to look at the kind of support equipment the person has in place.

- Presence of support equipment makes a huge difference to the success of therapy and patient recovery. Find out whether or not your patient has a walker that is well-matched to their specific abilities or walking needs.

- Recommend healthy lifestyle changes and adaptations to prevent further decline in bone and joint health. You can also suggest changes to make the patient's home safe. Interestingly, even simple changes in diet and lifestyle can help the patient restore, maintain and increase physical strength, balance, endurance, coordination,

Different Types of Geriatric Physical Therapy

Geriatric physical therapy is geared towards seniors and here's a brief description of the different types of therapy customized for older adults.

Exercise

Exercise programs include different forms of physical activity that helps seniors perform their daily tasks. These routines are specially designed to help improve the patient's muscle strength, bone density, physical endurance, energy, flexibility and more importantly, balance and coordination.

What sets a geriatric physical therapist apart is the fact that exercises are specially geared towards particular injury or condition. Physical activities such as stretching, walking, weight lifting and aquatic therapy help increase patient mobility and lessen the chances of injuries and fractures.

A geriatric physical therapist also educates the patient about the benefits of exercises. Some therapists share lots of great information and simple exercise older adults can perform themselves and continue with their exercise program at home.

Manual Therapy

Manual therapy focuses on improving the patient's circulation and restoring mobility. This type of therapy is more common after accidents and injury.

In addition to restoring blood circulation and mobility, manual therapy is also used for pain management. Manipulation of joints and muscles can reduce pain and make the patient feel better.

Education

Educating the patient is another important part of geriatric physical therapy. You've got to help patients understand how they can protect themselves from further injury.

Older adults are not very keen to follow their exercise program, but it is up to you to convince them. Older adults can follow simple exercises to feel better and enjoy a higher quality of life.

Geriatric physical therapists also teach patients about fall prevention, home safety and other "age related" changes that are often misunderstood.

The usual process of aging does lead to limitation of daily activities, however, pain and decreased physical mobility can easily be managed with regular exercise. You can be the complete source of information for body changes and how physical therapy can help patients regain lost abilities.

Neurological Physical Therapy

Neurological physical therapists are involved with patients who have a neurological disorder or disease. Individuals suffering from multiple sclerosis, spinal cord injury, cerebral palsy, Parkinson's diseases, Alzheimer's disease, brain injury, stroke and amyotrophic lateral sclerosis or Lou Gehrig's disease can benefit from neurological physical therapy and improve the overall quality of life.

Common problems of patients suffering from neurological conditions, particularly those mentioned above include poor balance, difficulty in movement, paralysis, poor vision and difficultly walking. Specialist neurological therapists work with patients who currently have a neurological disease or injury or have experienced it in the past.

Neurological disorders or conditions affect the nervous system and can happen in people from all age groups. Most people tend to suffer from neurological problems in the old age, but younger people can also develop these conditions.

Your spinal cord and brain control your body movements and sensations and neurological injuries and conditions lead to a loss of nerve function. Patients with neurological disorders are not able to perform certain activities which might get worse with time.

Stiffness of muscles and difficulty in walking or lifting things might continue to get worse as the disease progresses. If left untreated, patients may have trouble walking around and they may also experience additional health problems and an overall reduction in the quality of life.

What Neurological Physical Therapists Do

Neurological PTs design special treatments to relieve the symptoms and improve the quality of life for patients suffering from neurological disorder. Even after an injury or serious accident, cells that remain uninjured in the brain and spinal cord retain their ability to learn the functions that have been lost.

Neurological physical therapists have the knowledge related to human brain and spinal cord, therefore, can help patients walk and move again correctly. Most patients are able to move independently and enjoy life after a successful neurological physical therapy.

Neurological Physical Therapy and Multiple Sclerosis (MS)

Multiple sclerosis is a degenerative neurological disorder that affects people between the ages of 20 to 40. MS is also an inflammatory disease and the condition is more commonly seen in women than men. What makes MS so terrible is the fact that it involves a series of relapses and unpredictable prognosis.

People affected by multiple sclerosis experience physical disability which gets worse as the condition progresses. Other problems you can notice include difficulty in mobility, fatigue, improper balance and spasticity.

Neurological physiotherapist helps patient manage MS symptoms and retain functional abilities. Regular therapy also helps people improve balance and physical strength and lead an independent life.

Neurological PTs can come up with specific rehabilitation or self-management programs to improve levels of activity and quality of life in people with multiple sclerosis. Studies show that exercise can improve the health and well-being of patients suffering from multiple sclerosis.

Sports Physiotherapy

As you can guess, sports physiotherapy focuses on prevention, treatment, evaluation and rehabilitation of athletes or sports persons. Sports physical therapy plays an important part in performance enhancement of players, especially if they are involved with sports with challenging physical demands.

Players and athletes are also affected by injuries and other medical conditions and this has an impact on their ability to walk, move and even perform. Sports PTs use special equipment and exercises such as massages, body stretches to help players perform their best and manage pain and discomfort.

What Sports Physiotherapists Do

- In addition to treating athletes and other physically active individuals, sports PTs help performers stay active in their sports and prevent injuries.

- Sports PTs also develop exercise and training programs for players. Players prefer to have a customized program that suits their needs and helps them improve their physical strength and endurance.

- You'll also have to brace yourself for the unseen challenges. The job of a sports PT also involves moving injured players, treating muscle spasms and injuries and administering therapies on the field and all these duties are extremely stressful.

- Often sports PTs have to work with players who are frustrated with their condition and want quick results. A sports PT also needs to understand human psychology and behavior to come up with a solution that is acceptable to both parties.

Role of Physiotherapists in Sports – Some More Details

Sports physiotherapists don't just disappear off the field. They remain involved with sports and star performers and here's a brief description to give you a better idea.

Prevention and Treatment of Injuries

Athletes and performers train every day and this increases their chances of ending up with an injury. Sports PTs are present at routine trainings to help players prevent injuries. And if something unfortunate happens, the physiotherapist ensures safe and quick return to activity.

Players can prevent injuries by working on their physical strength and endurance and we would often find players seeking fitness advice and equipment recommendations from sports physiotherapist and trainers.

Treatment and prevention of injuries is one of the main focus areas of sports physical therapy. In a collective effort with physicians and healthcare providers, the sports physical therapists design and develop training and exercise programs for players of all ages.

Sports PTs work with star players and also help performers with chronic injuries and physical disabilities.

A sports physical therapist works with players to evaluate the different components of performance. Like other mishaps, sports injuries can lead to restricted or painful joint and muscle movement.

Muscle strains, fractured bones, ligament tear and other types of injuries can easily bring an active performer to the sidelines. Your job as a sports physical therapist is to design a recovery plan that suits the player.

You must consider individual player's strength, flexibility, range of motion, body posture and physical endurance before developing a plan. The treatment plan you design should be appropriate for the injuries your client (player) has sustained.

Every injury has a different plan of action and you can even combine different treatment strategies to speed up recovery and minimize damage.

A sports physical therapist will use a variety of treatments to treat a player and exercises are the key component in most cases. Other than exercise, sports PTs may use heat therapy, aquatic therapy, massages and other special techniques to improve muscle strength, balance, coordination and physical endurance.

The scope of treatment also depends on the severity of the injury. Some athletes have more serious injuries that require special attention.

For example, a sprinter with a twisted ankle needs to visit the physical therapist more regularly when compared to a table tennis player. Depending on the nature and severity of the injury, you'll have to determine how long the desired treatment will last and how will the workouts be spaced out the player progresses.

Performance Evaluation

Every player strives to excel and sports physical therapists are highly skilled in identifying factors that could boost player performance. A hallmark of this evaluation is the assessment of factors that could cause active and chronic injuries.

Sports physical therapists assist players to improve their performance in a number of different ways. The process may start with a thorough evaluation of the musculoskeletal and the cardiac system.

This basic evaluation will give you a clear idea about the physical strengths and weaknesses in an individual. You can then plan specific activities that are matched to the player's existing muscular strength, flexibility and physical endurance and will help them improve further.

Regular assessment and follow-up evaluations are important for further changes in the training program. Remember, you need to evaluate whether or not your training plan is achieving the desired results.

Education Requirements

Sports physical therapists need to complete a standard college degree as well as a master's degree in physical therapy. You can then apply for residency program in sports physical therapy. Remember, education and licensing regulations can vary depending on your country and state of residence, so check out your individual requirements from your local governing body.

The majority of licensed sports therapists work with sports clubs and athletes to get experience. You can also specialize in sports medicine programs after completing your degree in sports physiotherapy.

Career Forecast

Sports physiotherapy is one of most well paid professions and a rewarding and challenging career awaits you as a sports physical therapist. Sports physical therapy on the other hand also offers excellent job prospects and there is an increase in the total number of positions available. Opportunities are expected to increase across all physical therapy specialties, including sports physical therapy.

Women's Health Physiotherapy

This career is ideal for physiotherapists interested in managing women health issues. You'll be dealing with a range of clients of all ages.

Women health physiotherapy addresses issues related to sexual dysfunction, pelvic pain and urinary incontinence. While working with your female clients, you will be part of a number of important physiological events such as pregnancy, childbirth and the natural ageing process.

Those of you looking to enter the field of women health physiotherapy should also have a good understanding of cultural and behavioral issues related to women. This will definitely help you suggest better treatment options for common health problems affecting the female population.

What Women Health Physical Therapists Do?

Women health PTs address issues such as pelvic floor problems and urinary incontinence. Problems and complications related to the pelvic floor cause emotional distress and greatly reduce the quality of life. Being a specialist PT, it is your responsibility to help your clients enjoy social activities and be more confident.

Pelvic Floor Problems

The pelvic floor muscles play an important role in sexual function and help control your bladder and bowel movement.

Factors such as pregnancy, childbirth, menopause, pelvic surgery, obesity and natural ageing have a negative impact on the health and function of the pelvic floor muscles and they tend to become weak.

Normal pelvic floor function is essential for comfortable penetration and you need to relax the pelvic floor muscles to urinate and defecate.

Weakening of the pelvic floor is one of the main causes for bladder problems, pelvic pain, sexual dysfunction, uterine prolapse and bowel symptoms.

Women health physical therapists develop and design a pelvic floor exercise program that helps manage the conditions mentioned earlier. Each program is customized to the client's concerns and in most cases; these exercises are performed under the guidance of a trained physiotherapist.

Pelvic floor problems can become very distressing and complex if not treated at an early stage. Some women have difficulty in releasing their pelvic floor muscles which leads to pain in the bladder and lower abdomen.

Pregnancy and Post Natal Care

Pain in the pelvic girdle, hip or lower back is one of the most frequently reported complaints in expecting moms. Pelvic pain usually starts off during pregnancy, but it may also develop right after childbirth.

A number of physiological changes to the pelvic joints and muscles take place during pregnancy which may result in a weak or stressed pelvic floor. Targeted physical therapy is extremely useful in managing pelvic floor pain and symptoms that develop during pregnancy or after childbirth.

Your job as a women health physiotherapist will involve evaluating the exact cause(s) of pelvic pain, how you can manage the pain and more importantly, how you can prevent the symptoms from going bad to worse.

What Does Pregnancy and Post Natal Physiotherapy Involve?

As a women health PT, you will have to:

- Assess the joints and muscles of the spine, pelvis and hip.

- Design a customized exercise program to help your client strengthen the muscles and joint of the pelvic floor during pregnancy. You can also recommend the use of support taping or belt after discussion with a healthcare provider.

- Educate your clients about lifestyle and dietary changes that can help them manage pain and other pelvic floor symptoms.

- You'll also have to design a rehabilitation program following childbirth to prevent complications.

Lower back pain and neck pain are also very common during pregnancy. Women who are pregnant or recently had a baby suffer from constant lower back or neck pain which affects their daily life.

Majority of women face such issues because of hormonal and postural changes that occur during pregnancy. The increasing weight of the baby puts added stress on the pelvic joint and muscles, but specific physiotherapy treatments can relieve these symptoms and make pregnancy more comfortable.

What Women Health Physiotherapists Do Here

You'll have to assess the joints and muscles of the spine and core to get a clear idea about affected muscles and joints. You also need to recommend lifestyle changes, exercise program and activity modification to help clients strengthen the deep abdominal and pelvic floor muscles.

If you feel that the use of supportive belt or similar equipment is necessary, you can always have a discussion with a qualified obstetrician.

How Physical Therapy Can Help With Musculoskeletal Problems

Women health physical therapists have greater knowledge about muscles and joint issues related to women. Numerous physiological changes take place in the musculoskeletal system as a girl moves through different stages of life, i.e. from puberty to childbearing years and post menopause.

Often females experience pelvic floor muscle weakness and lower back pain during the prenatal and postpartum stages. Starting a physical therapy program early on prevents further complications after delivery.

Surprisingly, 1 in 3 expecting moms experience bladder dysfunction or poor bladder control after childbirth. Bladder leakage and control problems are emotionally disturbing and many women lose their self-confidence.

As mentioned earlier, pelvic floor muscles also play an important role in sexual function. Weakened or ineffective pelvic floor muscle system leads to vaginal heaviness and sexual pain. And these complications cause new moms to isolate themselves socially.

Chronic constipation, ageing, menopause, lifting heavy objects and pelvic surgery also cause pelvic floor muscles to weaken.

Studies show that customized pelvic floor exercise program (under supervision) during and after pregnancy helps keep pelvic floor muscles in good shape. As a women health PT, you can assist your clients in preventing and managing urinary leakage.

What Will Physiotherapy Involve In This Case?

You will be required to assess pelvic floor muscle function (PFM), which may also involve an internal vaginal examination. The result will help you design a customized exercise program based on your client's specific needs.

Like any other exercise program, your job as a PT would be to monitor the progress of your exercise program. It is important that you record and assess the progress of your designed plan like a sports physical therapist.

Physical Therapy and Managing Breastfeeding Problems

Breastfeeding moms are affected by problems like blocked ducts and mastitis which make breasts hard and painful to touch. Often women have a red lump or tender area on the breast and this has a negative impact on the bond moms share with their babies.

Therapeutic ultrasound is one effective physical treatment that can relieve painful breastfeeding problems. Physiotherapy for blocked ducts and mastitis also involves assessment of symptoms, breast tissue and breastfeeding history. You might have to work with lactation consultants and doctors if the case is too complicated.

How Women Health Physiotherapists Can Help Expecting Moms Prepare for Child Birth

Most moms-to-be are anxious about labor and wonder how their delivery would be like. Pregnancy does make people excited, but majority of expecting moms are really worried about labor pains.

As a women health PT, you can help mothers prepare their body for the birth of their baby. Advice and exercises especially related to the pelvic floor and abdominal muscles really helps during labor and reduces the need for extensive post natal care.

You can educate your clients about pelvic floor exercises, breathing techniques and relaxation methods for easy labor and faster physical recovery, especially of the pelvic floor.

Men's Health Physiotherapy

Surprisingly, not many men are aware that they have a pelvic floor and that they can experience problems like incontinence, sexual dysfunction and pelvic pain. Men's health physiotherapy is another emerging branch of physiotherapy which offers advice and treatment related to pelvic floor muscles problems in males.

Prostate Surgery and the Impact of Physical Therapy

Prostate surgery can be an emotional journey for men. Loss of bladder control haunts most patients and they are concerned how this surgery will influence their sexual life.

Fortunately, pelvic floor function can improve with physical therapy and you can help patients manage the severity of urine leakage after surgery. More importantly, regular pelvic floor exercises speeds up the recovery time and patients can achieve good bladder control fairly quickly.

Removal of the prostate does have a negative impact on bladder control, but pelvic floor exercises can compensate for this loss. You can instruct the patients to start the physical therapy or pelvic floor exercises before surgery to minimize the extent of bladder problems.

As a men's health PT, you can help patients that need to go to the toilet often or have accidental leakage of urine. Often patients have an overwhelming urge to go to the toilet which becomes quite distressing. Some patients feel that bladder problems interfere with their work and make life miserable.

Like women, the pelvic floor muscles in males play an important part in controlling bladder function. These muscles also support and control the bowel and are responsible for a satisfying sexual life.

Prostate surgery is not the only factor that negatively impacts the pelvic floor and bladder control. Chronic cough, obesity, ageing, pelvic surgery and constipation cause your pelvic floor muscles to weaken, but complications can be prevented by physical therapy.

Constipation and Physical Therapy

Constipation or uneasiness emptying your bowels is another common complaint you would come across a men's health physiotherapist. Poor diet, sedentary lifestyle, ageing and some medical conditions hinder complete defecation and leave you feeling uneasy, sluggish and bloated.

The muscles of your pelvic floor play an important part in complete bowel emptying and getting older, lifting heavy objects, chronic constipation and some types of surgery result in the pelvic floor muscles getting weak.

Physical therapy helps manage constipation and your job as a men's health PT will be to design a pelvic floor muscle exercise program (PFM) based on your patient's needs. For this, you need to assess the pelvic floor function first. Often this assessment will be accompanied by an internal rectal examination.

Physiotherapists are also required to educate the patient about emptying the bowels in a more effective way. You can also recommend dietary and lifestyle changes to help prevent constipation in the first place.

Physical Therapy and Erectile Dysfunction

Erectile dysfunction or the inability to achieve or maintain erections that are hard enough for penetration is very common in older men. However, the condition can also affect younger individuals.

Patients who find it difficult to get an erection are quite embarrassed about the situation and lose their self-esteem and sexual intimacy.

Erectile function or normal erection is a complex process and involves a number of factors. Emotional excitement, blood flow and the health of pelvic floor muscles play an important part in male sexual function and orgasm.

Men with weak pelvic floor muscles are most likely to have little or no erections and the condition gets worse with age.

Studies show that physiotherapy can help manage erectile dysfunction. You will be required to design a customized pelvic floor exercise plan that will help your patients improve erectile function and strengthen the pelvic floor.

Cardiovascular and Pulmonary Rehabilitation

Cardiovascular Physiotherapy, as the name suggests is the use of physiotherapy in the management of cardiovascular problems. Also known as respiratory physical therapy, this specialty area helps patients improve their cardiovascular system through regular training and exercise. The cardiovascular system comprises of the heart and blood vessels.

Cardiovascular diseases such as heart attack, stroke or angina can cause difficulties in blood flow and breathing. Patients also experience fatigue particularly after a cardiac surgery and there are chances of reoccurring or relapse of a stroke or heart attack.

Angina normally develops when there is a gradual buildup of plaque or fatty deposits in the arteries causing them to become narrow.

If a small piece of this fatty deposit cuts off the blood supply to the heart, i.e. forms a clot, it can result in heart attack. Stroke occurs when the clot cuts off the supply to the brain.

People suffering from heart conditions are more likely to develop other medical complications such as arthritis, diabetes, back pain and respiratory diseases including asthma.

Not many patients are aware of the fact that physiotherapy can help speed up recovery after cardiac surgery. On the other hand, people suffering from heart conditions can use physical therapy to manage their condition and prevent further complications.

What Cardiovascular Physical Therapists Do

You may work with patients with cardiac problems including chest pain, cardiomyopathy and victims of heart attack, stroke, angioplasty and bypass surgeries can also benefit from your expertise.

Physiotherapy can start within a couple of weeks after cardiac surgery; however, you have to administer a stress test to know how much exercise your patient can handle. Physical therapy after heart surgery involves walking on a treadmill or exercising on a stationary bike. Remember, you'll have to monitor the patient's vital signs very carefully during the physical therapy.

It is better to call cardiac surgery patients to an outpatient clinic or hospital for physical therapy. This way, you can gather and analyze medical information regarding the patient as well as monitor the person as they perform their exercises. You need to be alert and look for the smallest signs of troublesome symptoms during the course of physical therapy.

Once the patient gets better, you can educate the patients about gentle warm-up and stretching exercises they can do at home. Make sure you ask the patients to follow their customized exercise plan and report any problems they might have.

Physical therapy for heart conditions can continue for weeks and months and it is important that you monitor the progress of a patient.

Remember, if your plan isn't working, it is no use stick to the exercise schedule. You can recommend lifestyle and diet changes to help the patients recover and get into shape. After all, it is your responsibility to help the patient feel much healthier after physical therapy gets over.

Pulmonary rehabilitation consists of external mechanical maneuvers to mobilize and clear airway secretions. This type of physical therapy is recommended for patients who are unable to clear thick mucus and secretions from airways.

Examples include people suffering from lung abscess, pneumonia, bronchiectasis and cystic fibrosis. Some patients with neuromuscular disorders also need to undergo pulmonary rehabilitation.

As a respiratory therapist, you can use techniques such as postural drainage and chest percussion to remove mucus and other secretions. If physical maneuvers cause discomfort or the process is tiring for the patient, you can use mechanical vibrators and inflatable vests for the purpose. The method of airway clearance should be selected depending on patient's condition and needs.

Chest physiotherapy and pulmonary rehabilitation should never be used for patients with vertebral fractures, osteoporosis, rib fracture, recent hemoptysis and those on anticoagulation therapy.

What Respiratory Physical Therapists Do

- Reduce discomfort and disability of patients with chronic respiratory disease and improve their overall quality of life.

- Educate and train patients and caregivers about simple techniques to manage symptoms.

- Help patients take part in social and physical activities.

Needless to say, pulmonary rehabilitation techniques are selected depending on the need and unique considerations of a patient.

COPD and Pulmonary Rehabilitation

Chronic Obstructive Pulmonary Disease or COPD causes shortness of breath and limits the different types of activities people can do. Patients suffering from COPD cannot walk for long distances or even climb stairs. The worst part is that normal everyday life activities get harder with COPD.

Pulmonary rehabilitation for COPD patients includes a customized exercise program that people build their physical endurance and fitness. Respiratory physical therapists educate patients about different breathing techniques and strategies that could be used to perform normal activities with ease.

Pulmonary rehab exercises vary from patient to patient, but a typical COPD program can include both upper body and lower body exercises. Most physical therapists focus on leg workouts which include walking on a treadmill or a specially designed track. Some patients are also advised to perform more intense activities like stair climbing to build physical endurance.

Upper body workout for COPD patients involves breathing, arm and chest exercises. The muscles in the upper body, particularly in the chest are very important for breathing.

Patients are advised to breathe through a mouthpiece (against resistance) which increases the strength and endurance of the breathing muscles. Breathing exercises are very helpful for patients with very weak chest muscles.

Strength training is another important part of pulmonary rehabilitation. As a physiotherapist, you can add appropriate strength exercises to the rehab plan and help patients increase muscle strength and bulk.

Pediatric Physical Therapy

Pediatric physical therapists have a strong desire for working with children with movement dysfunction. Pediatric therapy is another recognized specialty area and people working as pediatric therapists are trained individuals who love working with children and their families.

What Pediatric Physical Therapists Do

The foremost foal of a pediatric PT is to help children achieve functional independence. You'll be responsible for improving physical strength and endurance in children. Plus, you also have to design exercise programs to promote health and wellness in young patients.

In addition to improving motor development and function, pediatric physical therapists also help enhance learning opportunities for children.

You would find pediatric PTs in hospitals and rehab centers. Moreover, many schools and community centers employ pediatric physical therapists to help children in early stages of development. Often PTs collaborate with parents, family and school authorities to develop and implement individualized programs for children.

You might have to enhance the child's physical strength and development by adapting daily activities. Even toys can be used to expand mobility options, however, you need to ensure that children use their equipment, toys effectively, and more importantly safely.

Children are more involved with their families so you might have to educate parents and families about their rehab needs. It's your job to help parents understand the specific healthcare needs of their kids.

Right before the start of the physical therapy, pediatric PTs interview the child's parents, teachers and healthcare provider to identify the basic needs. Next, they carry out a thorough medical examination and evaluation of the child to design a suitable program.

This evaluation process is focused on assessing the child's:

- Mobility

- Physical strength

- Cardiopulmonary function

- Endurance

- Joint function

- Muscle health

- Posture

- Balance and coordination

- Feeding pattern

- Motor skills

- Speech pattern

- Neuromotor development

- Sensory development

Children may receive pediatric physical therapy in hospitals and PT clinic. Physical therapy is administered when the child is receiving medical care for a related condition or during acute care episode.

Chapter 3: Step In the Real World of Physiotherapy

Becoming a physiotherapist and completing degree programs is just the beginning. You have to step in the real world of physiotherapy and build on the broad base of professional education.

Resume Building

Your Resume is Your Most Valuable Tool

Your resume is one of the most valuable tools when you're looking for a job and there are a few things you need to get right when it comes to your CV. There is no room for mistakes, but what could be the worst resume mistake you could make?

The first thing you need to see is that your resume should be targeted to the job market you're looking for. Neglecting important keywords or failing to list your achievements can cost you greatly, especially if you're looking to enter into the world of physiotherapy.

Having said this, it is important that you avoid being sloppy while putting together your resume. You need to look for simple spelling and punctuation mistakes. Forgetting basic grammar rules or sending your resume in the wrong format perhaps is the most unprofessional thing to do. You shouldn't be surprised if your CV doesn't get one call because it had tons of spelling and grammar issues.

What would be a smart thing to do while drafting your resume? First, don't rely entirely on your word processing software as no software can fix "mistakes" on your CV. Make sure your qualification is spelled correctly and that you have written all the necessary details.

Another good thing to do is list the information on a sheet of paper, go over the draft several times, and then catch the errors. You can proofread your final draft yourself or get a few more "pairs" to spot the mistakes you've made (if any).

Customize Your Resume to the Field You're Applying For

Generic physiotherapist CV doesn't impress any employer. You might get an entry level job with a generic "one size fits all" CV, but you'll have to do lots of hard work to advance in your career.

For example, if you're a specialist respiratory physical therapist, it is important that your CV highlights your qualification. You'll have more chances of going through the initial screening process and the employer would definitely consider you as a good "hire."

It's always good to use the keywords listed in the job ads you're applying for. And for this, you need to tweak your generic CV just a little bit and become the best fit for your new employer.

Not to forget, you need to send your CV in the correct format. If your employer asks you to fill an online form, make sure you read the details correctly and recheck the form before submitting it. If the job listing clearly states "email your CV", make sure you send your application and cover letter via email and follow other instructions mentioned carefully.

For example, if you're sending your CV to an employer email directly, try inserting your CV within the body of the e-mail itself. You can also attach a "document" version with fancier layout, just in case your employer needs to "show" your resume to other staff.

How You Can Make Your CV Stand Out

It is necessary that your CV is easy to read and your employer can scan important details quickly and effectively. Try listing information under different sections, preferably under "clear section headings."

Stick to bullet points and break large chunks of text into more digestible "bite-size" chunks. Remember, your CV should list all the important details and it should be uncluttered and eye-catching. As mentioned earlier, you also need to check for spelling and grammatical errors.

Effective resume has a professional objective, i.e. you need to mention your intended future path. Also, take out time to scan your education and achievements and summarize them under your "professional profile."

Remember, your sentences should flow seamlessly and avoid cliché or extremely wordy sentences at all costs. Even if you write a few lines, it should encourage your reader (employer) to read your complete CV.

It's good to be persuasive to grab reader's attention, but don't over the board. The worst mistake you can make is to write something you cannot fulfill.

Adding an "achievement" section on your CV can increase your CV power quite dramatically. Of course, your employer would be interested to know more about areas you've excelled and how you can achieve similar results in your new job position. This is nothing less than an opportunity to advertise your skills, and you should use it skillfully.

Needless to say, an effective resume should be concise and "to-the-point." In general, your resume should be informative, but not longer than two A4 pages. It is best to include information which will help you "sell" your skills, but don't include details that are irrelevant to your new job or position.

If possible, you should customize your CV according to the specific job and organization you are applying. The reason is quite simple. If you match your skills to the specific needs of the job and organization, you can achieve greater success. Hiring managers have to review piles of CVs every day and they want to select the best person for the job. Make sure your CV makes the final cut even if there's just one opening.

Before you start editing your entire resume, just have a look at some of the advertised physical therapist positions on popular jobsites.

Even though the task looks daunting, it will give you a clear idea about the kind of employee employers are seeking. Simply put, you'll have a better understanding of the skills, experience, traits and qualities. Most job ads clearly mention requirements like background in pediatrics or acute care experience, which should make your CV writing task easier.

Another common mistake most people do is to ignore "soft skills" such as excellent interpersonal skills or energetic team player. Interestingly, your employer is also keen to know more about you as a person, so feature your personal traits in addition to your qualification and place of employment.

What Your Resume Should Contain:

Summary

The opening paragraph of your resume should feature your key strengths and qualifications. Don't forget to include your objective at the start followed by your key degrees, certifications and experience. If you have worked with special patients, don't forget to include it under the summary section.

Here's an example summary section for a pediatric physical therapist.

Licensed pediatric physical therapist with ten of experience providing inpatient and outpatient rehabilitative services for infants and children

Master of Science in Physical Therapy and additional credentials include <XYZ> certifications

An excellent team player with a strong reputation for effective communication skills

Qualifications and certifications

Hiring managers want to know what you have done along with how well you have performed over the years. Write your resume in a way that employers can quickly grasp your key skills and contributions.

Achievements

As mentioned earlier, a small achievement section can increase the worth of your CV quite dramatically.

You can include:

- Patient success stories

- Special cases you've handled

- Work settings

- Rehab treatments you've supervised

- Contributions you made

- Any special technology or equipment you've used

- Recognition and rewards you've received for your outstanding performance

Membership of a professional body also helps you show dedication to the field. You can list the details of your membership in the affiliation section.

Keywords

Your resume should contain keywords that are relevant to the physical therapy industry. For example, you should include specific job titles, degrees, certifications, names of professional organizations and areas of specialty. If you're using an abbreviation on your resume, list the complete word as well. This will help your employer understand the information you've listed.

Remember, your resume should immediately grab an employer's attention, so make sure you customize your objective and qualification section to address the employer's specific needs. When you show you're a good fit in the employer's team, your resume will stand out from the crowd quite easily.

Internship/Apprenticeship

A career in the field of physical therapy is ideal for those who are interested in kinesiology, the science of human movement. Physiotherapy can certainly be a demanding and stressful job especially if you're new to the field, but things will get better as you become more familiar with your new career.

Internships and apprenticeships can lead to greater job satisfaction as you would know the "real" implementation of the course you've learned. You'll have a better idea of how you should interact with patients and what you should expect as a physiotherapist.

If you're interested in entering the field of physiotherapy, you should definitely look for an internship during the education years.

You'll not only get a chance to work under an experienced, licensed physical therapist, but you can also understand the skills and knowledge you've just learned.

Internship will give you a chance to create a treatment plan with a senior PT and interact with the patient directly. What's better than gaining first-hand learning experience when you're studying and you have an experienced professional to offer guidance and advice.

You'll definitely get some experience in assessing patients and treatment plans and the best part is that you can see the results if the treatment methods in real-time.

For example, you can assess the effectiveness of pulmonary rehabilitation methods in the hospital or rehab center where your internship occurs. You'll also have access to the latest treatment methods and equipment and this will help you after you become a licensed physical therapist and want to help your own patients.

The extent to which you will be involved in the treatment method depends on the organization offering the internship and the personal choice of patients.

Even if you don't get a chance to assist or perform the treatment method directly, you'll still be in the best position to learn new things. It's not wrong to say that you might find yourself working with the latest equipment and technology or the most critically advanced pathologies.

There are plenty of perks to be gained from simple internships and anything that helps you gain experience and polish your skills would definitely pay you well.

Remember, an internship that really tests your emotions, abilities and skills at an early stage would be of great help when you're actually working with patients.

You can contact your local hospitals, rehab centers and other PT settings to learn more about opportunities that are available.

Job Hunting

Impressing a potential employer is not really simple even if you have the right qualifications and experience for the job. You have to present your skills the right way to convince your employer, but before that, your job hunting skills need to be really impressive.

If you've just started looking for a job, you have to be consistent and patient. There would be times when you would be really depressed, but you don't have to give up. Show that you love your profession and you have a great level of commitment. Keep trying hard and you should definitely succeed.

Job hunting process is one of the best learning phases of your life. There's a time and place to do everything and you might find yourself in awkward positions. The key to success, however is sticking to your good things. You've spend so much time learning about physical therapy and you should be able to work things out for yourself. Getting hired means that you have to exceed your own as well as your employer's expectations.

It's always good to surprise your employer with your resume and make promises you can keep. If you feel you can add value to a project, go ahead and grab the opportunity with both hands.

As mentioned earlier, physical therapists work in many different settings including hospitals, nursing homes and private clinics. The American Physical Therapy Association website provides job listings for physical therapists that are regularly updated.

You can visit the website to know more about the job openings that are available. Online jobsites, local newspapers and career fairs are also good places to look for a job in physical therapy. Online jobsites allow you to search for jobs based on your preferences, i.e. your specialty, organization or place of residence.

State Registration and Licensure

Physical therapists in the United States can only practice or work in a state in which they have a valid license. The process of obtaining a license varies from state to state, but you need to pass the National Physical Therapy Exam and a state test. Once you pass the exams, your application will be reviewed and approved by the state organization that regulates health care.

If you want to work in more than one state or want to transfer your job, you must successfully pass the National Exam and state test in both locations. Most locations in the United States require licensed physical therapists to renew their license. This renewal process is applicable after every two years. You'll have to complete the prescribed number of education courses/units as per your state laws. The number of education units also varies from state to state.

Some states do not require education units and in some cases, you can renew your license by taking online courses or attending seminars. Simply put, please refer to your state authority for latest information on license requirements.

Most physical therapists in the UK go through *British Association of Counseling and Psychotherapy* development, theory and practical work to become a certified physical therapist. BACP certification is fast becoming one of the essential requirements of employers looking for specialist PTs in the UK.

Final Words

At the end of this useful resource, you would be familiar with the requirements to begin working as a physical therapist. You know what physical therapists do, how much they can earn and more importantly, what are the education requirements to start working as a PT. Best of luck for your career and here's hoping that your journey is successful.

Helpful Resources

www.apta.org

http://www.csp.org.uk/

http://www.bacp.co.uk/

www.physiotherapyboard.gov.au

www.physiocouncil.com.au

Glossary

Advanced GSVQ

Abbreviation for General Scottish Vocational Qualification.

Advanced GNVQ

Abbreviation for **General National Vocational Qualification**. These qualifications relate to occupational areas in general, rather than any specific job. GNVQ could be taken in a wide range of subjects.

Alzheimer's disease

A progressive degenerative disease of the brain that leads to dementia. In the brain, Alzheimer's disease involves degeneration of the cortical regions, especially the frontal and temporal lobes. There is currently no cure for Alzheimer's disease, but new medications and therapies appear to slow its progress and improve the patient's ability to function.

American Physical Therapy Association (APTA)

Headquartered in Alexandria, Virginia, APTA represents approximately 76,000 physiotherapy members throughout the United States. Being a national professional organization, APTA's goal is to foster advancements in physical therapy practice, research, and education.

Amyotrophic Lateral Sclerosis

Amyotrophic lateral sclerosis is a rapidly progressive, invariably fatal neurological disease that attacks the nerve cells responsible for controlling voluntary muscles.

Anatomy

A branch of morphology that deals with the structure of organisms.

Angina

A disease marked by spasmodic attacks of intense suffocative pain.

Apprenticeship

Apprenticeship is a combination of on-the-job training (OJT) and related classroom instruction under the supervision of a journey-level craft person or trade professional in which workers learn the practical and theoretical aspects of a highly skilled occupation.

After completing an apprenticeship program, the worker's journey-level status provides an additional benefit of nationwide mobility at journey level scale.

Aquatic Therapy

The exercising of muscle groups under water, which increases range-of-motion and light resistance for rehabilitation.

Australian Physiotherapy Association

The **Australian Physiotherapy Association** (APA), which has a branch in every state and territory, is the professional body for physiotherapists in Australia. The organization has more than 14000 members and over 300 members in volunteer positions on committees or working parties. The Australian Physiotherapy Association is also a member of the World Confederation for Physical Therapy (WCPT).

BACP Certification

British Association for Counselling and Psychotherapy (BACP) is the largest professional body representing counseling and psychotherapy in the UK. BACP certification shows that the person is dedicated to practicing responsibly, ethically and to the highest of standards.

Bone Mineral Density

Bone Mineral Density is a medical term normally referring to the amount of **mineral** per square centimeter of bones. It reflects the strength of bones as represented by calcium content. A **Bone Mineral Density** (BMD) test measures the **mineral density** (such as calcium) in bones using a special X-ray or computed tomography (CT) scan.

Bronchiectasis

Bronchiectasis is a condition in which an area of the bronchial tubes is permanently and abnormally widened (dilated), with accompanying infection.

BTEC National Diploma

BTEC stands for Business & Technology Education Council. The BTEC National Diploma is a vocational qualification at Level 3 in England, Wales and Northern Ireland and is equivalent to three A-Levels.

Cardiomyopathy

Cardiomyopathy is a chronic disease of the heart muscle (myocardium), in which the muscle is abnormally enlarged, thickened, and/or stiffened.

Cardiopulmonary Function

Cardiopulmonary function is the interrelationship between the workings of the heart and lungs.

Cardiothorasic

Related to or involving the heart and chest.

Cerebral Palsy

Cerebral palsy is a disorder of movement, muscle tone or posture that is caused by an insult to the immature, developing brain, most often before birth.

Chronic Injury

Chronic injury refers to the sort of physical injury that develops slowly and is persistent and long-lasting.

Clinical Biomechanics

Biomechanics is the study of the structure and function of biological systems. Clinical biomechanics is a branch of biomechanics that applies physical principles to treat patients.

Commission on Accreditation in Physical Therapy Education (CAPTE)

The Commission on Accreditation in Physical Therapy Education (CAPTE) is an accrediting agency that is nationally recognized by the US Department of Education (USDE) and the Council for Higher Education Accreditation (CHEA). CAPTE grants specialized accreditation status to qualified entry-level education programs for physical therapists and physical therapist assistants.

COPD

Chronic Obstructive Pulmonary Disease (COPD) is a lung disease characterized by chronic obstruction of lung airflow that interferes with normal breathing and is not fully reversible.

CV

Curriculum Vitae, CV is a written description of your work experience, educational background and skills.

Cystic Fibrosis

Cystic fibrosis is a hereditary chronic disease of the exocrine glands. It is characterized by the production of viscid mucus that obstructs the pancreatic ducts and bronchi, leading to infection and fibrosis.

Electromyography/Electromyogram Test

An electromyogram (EMG) is a test that is used to record the electrical activity of muscles. Muscles produce electrical current during activity and this current is usually proportional to the level of the muscle activity. An EMG is also referred to as a myogram.

EMGs can be used to detect abnormal electrical activity of muscle that can occur in many diseases and conditions, including muscular dystrophy, inflammation of muscles, pinched nerves, peripheral nerve damage, ALS and many others.

Electrotherapy

Electrotherapy is the use of electrical energy as a medical treatment.

Electrophysiology

Electrophysiology is the biomedical field dealing with the study of electric activity in the body. Electrophysiology includes the study of the production of electrical activity and the effects of that electrical activity on the body.

Erectile Dysfunction

Erectile dysfunction or ED is the inability to achieve penile erection or to maintain an erection until ejaculation. It is also called impotence.

Fellowship

A fellowship is the period of training that a professional may undertake after completing a specialty training program (residency). After completing a fellowship in the relevant sub-specialty, the professional is allowed to practice without direct supervision by other professionals in that sub-specialty. Fellowship is a common practice in medicine.

Health and Care Professions Council (HCPC)

The Health and Care Professions Council (HCPC) is a statutory regulator of more than 300,000 health and care professionals from 16 professions in the United Kingdom. The Council was set up in 2003 under the National Health Service Reform and Health Care Professions Act 2002, to replace the Council for Professions Supplementary to Medicine (CPSM).

Heart Attack

Heart attack is damage to an area of heart muscle that is deprived of oxygen. This is usually due to blockage of a diseased coronary artery. Heart attack is typically accompanied by chest pain radiating down one or both arms. The severity of the heart attack varies with the extent and location of the damage.

Heat Therapy

Heat therapy or thermotherapy is the application of heat to the body for pain relief. The treatment methods use hot cloth, hot water, ultrasound, heating pad, hydrocollator packs, whirlpool baths and cordless FIR heat therapy wraps.

The beneficial effects of heat therapy include improved collagen tissue health, reduced joint stiffness, reduced pain, relieved muscle spasms, reduced inflammation, increased healing and increased blood flow.

Hemoptysis

Hemoptysis is spitting up blood or blood-stained sputum from the respiratory tract. It occurs when tiny blood vessels that line the lung airways are broken.

HND

A Higher National Diploma (HND) is a higher education qualification of the United Kingdom. It is roughly equivalent to the first two years of a 3 year degree (with honors), or to the Diploma of Higher Education. An HND takes two years of full-time study, or one year full-time following successful completion of a Higher National Certificate; part-time study takes longer.

Hospice Care

Care designed to give supportive care to people in the final phase of a terminal illness and focus on comfort and quality of life, rather than cure. The goal is to enable patients to be comfortable and free of pain, so that they live each day as fully as possible.

Incontinence

Unable to restrain natural discharges or evacuations of urine or feces.

Internship

Internship is any official or formal program to provide practical experience for beginners in an occupation or profession. For example, an internship program for physical therapists.

Kinesiology

Also known as human kinetics, it is the scientific study of human movement.

Licensure

Licensure is granting of permission by a competent authority, especially to engage in professional practice.

Lung Abscess

Lung abscess is an acute or chronic infection of the lung, marked by a localized collection of pus, inflammation, and destruction of tissue.

Mastitis

Mastitis is the inflammation of breast tissue.

Menopause

The period of permanent cessation of menstruation, it usually occurs between the ages of 45 and 55.

Multiple Sclerosis

A "demyelinating" disease marked by patches of hardened tissue in the brain or the spinal cord and associated especially with partial or complete paralysis and jerking muscle tremor.

Muscle Spasm

Persistent involuntary tension in one or more muscles usually of central origin and commonly associated with pain and excessive irritability.

Musculoskeletal

Related to or involving both muscles and skeleton.

National Exam US

The Federation of State Boards of Physical Therapy (FSBPT) administers the National Physical Therapy Examination (NPTE), the examination that every graduate of a physical therapy or physical therapist assistant education program must pass to become a licensed physical therapist or licensed/certified physical therapist assistant (or to regain licensure/certification if lapsed) in the United States (US).

Neuromuscular

Jointly involving nerves and muscles.

Neurological Disease

Structural, biochemical or electrical disorder or abnormality in the brain, spinal cord and nerves.

Neuroscience

Neuroscience is the scientific study of the nervous system.

Obstetrician

A physician who specializes in obstetrics, a branch of medical science that deals with childbirth.

Osteoarthritis

A type of arthritis marked by degeneration of the cartilage and bone of joints.

Parkinson's Disease

A progressive chronic disorder of the central nervous system characterized by impaired muscular coordination and tremor.

Pharmacology

The science that deals with drugs including their origin, composition, pharmacokinetics, therapeutic use, and toxicology.

Physical Therapy

See physiotherapy.

Physiotherapist

Physical Therapists or physiotherapists are primary health-care professionals who are experts in movement and function of the body. A physiotherapist works with people who have become disabled by injury, illness, or age.

Physiotherapy

Physiotherapy is the evaluation, diagnosis, and treatment of a condition with physical methods such as exercise, massage, aquatic therapy, etc.

Physical Therapist

See physiotherapist.

Physiology

The branch of biology dealing with the functions and activities of living organisms and their parts, including all physical and chemical processes.

Pneumonia

Pneumonia is an infection that inflames the lungs' air sacs. The air sacs may fill up with fluid or pus, causing symptoms such as a cough with mucus, fever and chills.

Post Menopause

After menopause, i.e. the period of time after a woman has experienced 12 consecutive months without menstruation.

Postpartum

The period of time following childbirth.

Prenatal

Previous to birth or giving birth.

Prognosis

A forecasting of the probable course and outcome of a disease, especially of the chances of recovery.

Prostate

A gland within the male reproductive system that is located just below the bladder. The function of the prostate is to secrete a slightly alkaline milky or white fluid that usually makes up 50–75% of the volume of the semen.

Puberty

The condition of being or the period of becoming first capable of reproducing sexually marked by maturing of the genital organs and development of secondary sex characteristics.

Registration

The act of registering to regulate the practice of physical therapy.

Residency

Residency is a stage of graduate medical training. A physical therapy resident practices under the supervision of fully licensed PTs usually in a hospital or clinic. The residency can be followed by a fellowship.

Resume

A brief account of one's professional or work experience and qualifications.

Rheumatoid Arthritis

Inflammation of a joint or joints, characterized by pain and stiffness of the affected parts.

Spinal Stenosis

Spinal stenosis is an abnormal narrowing of the spinal canal that may occur in any of the regions of the spine.

Sternocleidomastoid Muscles

Either of two muscles of the neck that serve to flex and rotate the head.

Stroke

A stroke is the sudden death of brain cells in a localized area due to inadequate blood flow.

Spasticity

Spasticity or **muscular hypertonicity** is a disorder of the body motor system, and especially the central nervous system (CNS), in which certain muscles are continuously contracted. This contraction causes stiffness or tightness of the muscles and may interfere with movement and speech.

Torticollis

A condition in which the neck is twisted and the head inclined to one side. It is caused by spasmodic contraction of the muscles of the neck.

The US Department Of Labor

A U.S government cabinet body responsible for standards in occupational safety, wages and number of hours worked.

Uterine Prolapse

The falling down or slipping of the uterus from its usual position.

Index

COPD (62, 84)

CV (67, 68, 69, 70, 71, 72, 84)

Cystic Fibrosis (61, 84)

Electromyography/Electromyogram Test (33, 85)

Electrotherapy (33, 34, 85)

Electrophysiology (33, 34, 85)

Erectile Dysfunction (58, 85)

Fellowship (35, 85)

Health and Care Professions Council (HCPC) (23, 86)

Heart Attack (59, 60, 86)

Heat Therapy (46, 86, 87)

Hemoptysis (61, 87)

HND (18, 87)

Hospice Care (27, 87)

Incontinence (36, 49, 56, 87)

Internship (24, 74, 75, 88)

Kinesiology (24, 88)

Licensure (2, 78, 89)

Lung Abscess (61, 88)

Mastitis (54, 88)

Menopause (50, 52, 53, 88)

Notes:

CPSIA information can be obtained at www.ICGtesting.com
Printed in the USA
LVOW01s2050050215

425858LV00028B/1269/P